Learning Short-take®

RECRUITING FOR RESULTS

Secrets of selecting the right person for the job

CATHERINE MATTISKE

TPC - The Performance Company Pty Ltd
Level 20, Darling Park
Tower 2, 201 Sussex Street,
Sydney NSW 2000
Australia

ACN 077 455 273
email: tpc@tpc.net.au
Website: www.catherinemattiske.com

© TPC – The Performance Company Pty Limited
First edition published in 2006
Second edition published in 2011
Third edition published in 2022

All rights reserved. Apart from any fair dealing for the purposes of study, research or review, as permitted under Australian copyright law, no part of this publication may be reproduced by any means without the written permission of the copyright owner. Every effort has been made to obtain permission relating to information reproduced in this publication.

The information in this publication is based on the current state of commercial and industry practice, applicable legislation, general law and the general circumstances as at the date of publication. No person shall rely on any of the contents of this publication and the publisher and the author expressly exclude all liability for direct and indirect loss suffered by any person resulting in any way from the use of or reliance on this publication or any part of it. Any options and advice are offered solely in pursuance of the author's and the publisher's intention to provide information, and have not been specifically sought.

For eBook version: By payment of the required fees, you have been granted the non-exclusive, non-transferable right to access and read the text of this e-book on screen. No part of this text may be reproduced, transmitted, downloaded, decompiled, reverse engineered, or stored in or introduced into any information storage retrieval system, in any form or by any means, whether the electronic or mechanical, now known or hereinafter invented, without the express permission of the author.

 A catalogue record for this book is available from the National Library of Australia

National Library of Australia
Cataloguing-in-Publication data

Mattiske, Catherine
Recruiting for Results: Secrets of Selecting the Right Person for the Job

ISBN 978-1-921547-28-7

1. Occupational training 2. Learning I. Title

370.113

Distributed by TPC - The Performance Company - www.catherinemattiske.com
For further information contact TPC - The Performance Company, Sydney Australia on +61 (02) 9555 1953.

HELLO.

Welcome to the Learning Short-take® process!

This Learning Short-take® is a bite sized learning package that aims to improve your skills and provide you with an opportunity for personal and professional development to achieve success in your role.

This Learning Short-take® combines self study with workplace activities in a unique learning system to keep you motivated and energized.
So let's get started!

Step 1:
What's inside?

- Learning Short-take®. This section contains all of the learning content and will guide you through the learning process.
- Learning Activities. You will be prompted to complete these as you read through.
- Learning Journal. This is a summary of your key learnings. Update it when prompted.
- Skill Development Action Plan. Learning is about taking action. This is your action plan where you'll plan how you will implement your learning.

Step 2:
Complete the Learning Short-take®

- Learning Short-takes® are best completed in a quiet environment that is free of distractions.
- Schedule time in your calendar to complete the Learning Short-take® and prioritize this time as an investment in your own professional development.
- Depending on the title, most participants complete the Learning Short-take® from 90 minutes to 2.5 hours.

Step 3:
Meet with your Manager/Coach

- Schedule a 30 minute meeting with your Manager or Coach.
- At this meeting share your completed Activities, Learning Journal and Skill Development Action Plan.
- Most importantly, discuss and agree on how you will implement your learning in your role.

GET VIP ACCESS
TO YOUR MATERIALS

This Learning Short-take® includes an interactive activity book, associated tools and job aids, plus a bonus eBook.

1 Visit
https://www.catherinemattiske.com/books

2 Select your book

3 Click: **VIP ACCESS**

4 Enter the code: RFR2022337

WELCOME

Recruiting for Results
Secrets of Selecting the Right Person for the Job

Recruiting for Results combines self-study with realistic workplace activities to provide managers with the key skills and techniques to recruit and select the right employees for an organization. You will learn to deliver cost savings to the business by employing the right people, reducing employee turnover and re-recruitment costs, and achieving organizational results.

The recruitment of good employees is critical to long term business survival and should be treated as a competitive and strategic activity. **Recruiting for Results** will provide you with the skills to find the best people to fit the culture of your organization and contribute to its goals from writing the position description to powerful interviewing techniques.

Recruiting for Results includes the **Candidate Assessment Summary, Candidate Profile, Interview Report Form**, and the **Position Description**. They are provided as free downloadable tools.

Now let's get started!

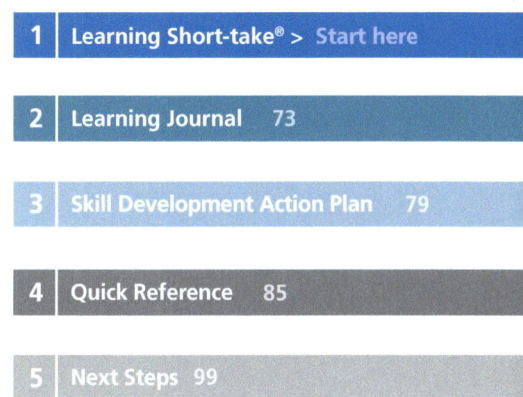

1 | Learning Short-take® > Start here
2 | Learning Journal 73
3 | Skill Development Action Plan 79
4 | Quick Reference 85
5 | Next Steps 99

"If you suspect a man, don't employ him, and if you employ him, don't suspect him."

CHINESE PROVERB

"

"Hire people who are better than you are, then leave them to get on with it... Look for people who will aim for the remarkable, who will not settle for the routine."

DAVID OGILVY

Section 1

LEARNING SHORT-TAKE®

WHAT'S IN THIS LEARNING SHORT-TAKE®

"To select the wrong person for a job is a common mistake; not to remove him/her is a fatal weakness."

AUTHOR UNKNOWN

Table of Contents

How to Complete Your Learning Short-take®	5
Activity Checklist	6
Learning Objectives	7
Let's Get Started	8
Part 1 - Getting Started	9
Recruitment Overview	10
The Recruitment & Selection Process	12
Part 2 - The Need to Recruit	15
Establishing the Need to Recruit	16
Determining the Requirements of the Position	21
Part 3 - Sourcing Employees	29
Internal Sources of Employees	30
External Sources of Employees	35
Part 4 - The Interviewing Process	43
The Interview Process	44
The Importance of Listening in Interviews	57
Part 5 - The Selection Process	61
The Selection Decision	62
Part 6 - Tips and Traps	67
Eight Hiring Mistakes Employers Make: From Application to Interview	68

HOW TO COMPLETE YOUR LEARNING SHORT-TAKE®

1. **Reflect on your skills and abilities** in managing the recruitment process, and how well you use these skills to attract and select the best candidates.

2. **Complete the Initial Skills Self-Assessment.**

3. Highlight specific skill areas that you believe you could develop more. Add these to the **Learning Journal.** Add to your Learning Journal as you go.

4. When you have completed this Learning Short-take® **meet with your Manager/Coach.** In this meeting, you will jointly establish a personal **Skill Development Action Plan.**

5. **Subject to your coach's final review** and assessment, you will either sign off the module, or undertake further skill development as appropriate.

"Dig your well, before you're thirsty."

HARVEY MACKAY

ACTIVITY CHECKLIST

"When you hire people that are smarter than you are, you prove you are smarter than they are."

R. H. GRANT

During this Learning Short-take® you will be prompted to complete the following activities:

- Activity 1 -   Initial Skills Self-Assessment   13
- Activity 2 -   Terms & Definitions Match   19
- Activity 3a - Create a Position Description   25
- Activity 3b - Candidate Profile   27
- Activity 4a - Internal Recruitment Advertising   41
- Activity 4b - Growing the External Talent Pool   42
- Activity 5 -   Developing Interview Questions   56
- Activity 6 -   Interview Report Form   59
- Activity 7 -   Candidate Assessment Summary   63
- Activity 8 -   From Hiring Mistakes to Hiring Greats   71
- Learning Journal   73
- Skill Development Action Plan   79

LEARNING OBJECTIVES

After you have completed this Learning Short-take®, you should be able to:

- Outline the purpose of recruitment.
- Identify the steps in the recruitment process.
- Explain how to establish a recruitment need.
- Develop effective Position Descriptions and Candidate Profiles.
- Identify the various sources of employees (internal and external).
- Explain key principles of interviewing and candidate selection.
- List eight common recruitment mistakes.
- List 10 tips for recruiting success.
- Create a Skill Development Action Plan.

"Time spent on hiring is time well spent."

ROBERT HALF,
AMERICAN BUSINESSMAN

LET'S GET STARTED

The recruitment of good employees is critical to long term business survival and should be a treated as a competitive and strategic activity. Finding the best people to fit your organizational culture and contribute to the goals of the company is both a challenge and an opportunity.

The war for talent is on, and the candidate market is tight. Recruitment cannot afford to be a reactive process that takes place when employees leave. In order to be successful, recruitment must be about pro-actively anticipating trends in employee turnover and changes to the strategic direction of the organization. Workforce planning is as critical as sales, marketing and financial planning.

This Learning Short-take® combines self-study with workplace activities to provide you with the key skills and techniques to recruit and select the right employees for your organization. You will learn to deliver cost savings to the business by employing the right people, reducing employee turnover and re-recruitment costs, and achieving organizational results. The Learning Short-take® is designed for completion in approximately 90 minutes.

GETTING STARTED

PART 1

RECRUITMENT OVERVIEW

Purpose of Recruitment

The fundamental goal of recruitment is to ensure that the organization is effectively and efficiently staffed at all times. The purpose of the recruitment process is to attract suitable people to apply for employment vacancies, and to successfully match candidates with the specific requirements of the job and the organization. Effective recruiting is about attracting and selecting the right candidates who will deliver performance results.

Costs of Recruitment

Recruitment can be an expensive process. The cost of recruitment, both in real and hidden terms can be enormous. Generally speaking it costs 20% of an individual's total salary package for an advertised recruitment campaign. This increases to 30% for executive searches and the involvement of recruitment agencies.

These figures do not include the hidden costs of recruitment such as:

- loss of productivity as the new employee learns.
- formal training for the new employee.
- time to interview applicants.
- temporary staff until permanent staff are appointed.
- turnover of new staff in the first year.

The Recruitment Iceberg

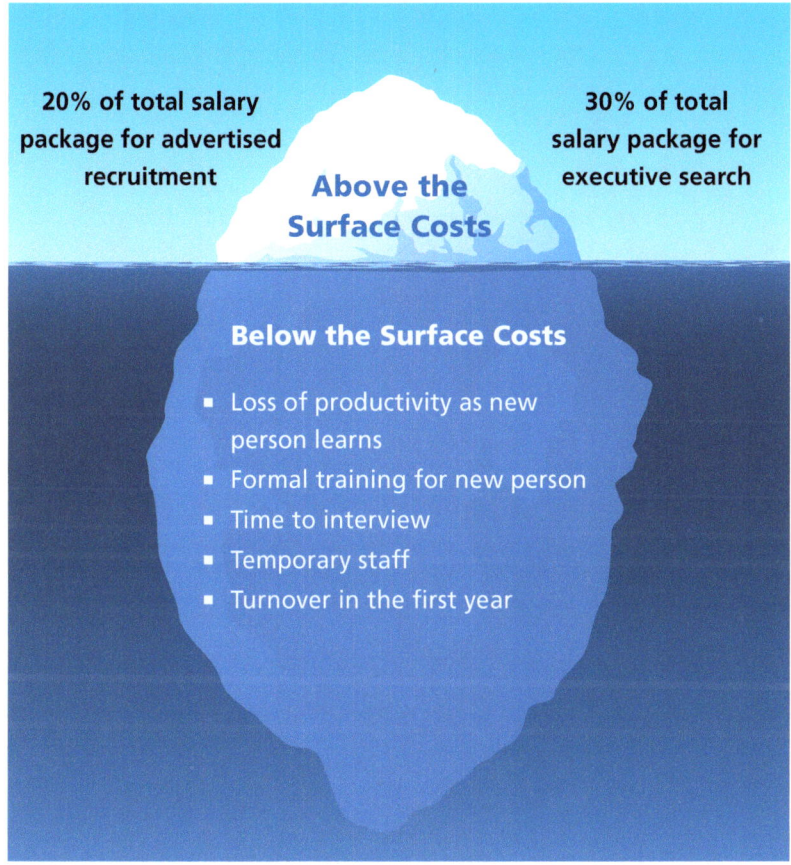

The high costs of recruitment can be minimized by conducting each stage of the recruitment process effectively.

THE RECRUITMENT AND SELECTION PROCESS

```
Vacancy Occurs
      ▼
Establish the Need to Recruit
      ▼
Review Position Description/Candidate Profile.
Establish Employment Arrangements/Conditions.
      ▼
Source Candidates Internal/External, Advertising,
Use of Recruitment Consultants
      ▼
Pre-Selection against Position Description/Candidate Profile
      ▼
Interview Preparation
      ▼
Interview and Candidate Assessment
      ▼
Selection
      ▼
Appointment
```

Complete Activity # 1
Initial Skills Self-Assessment

ACTIVITY 1: INITIAL SKILLS SELF-ASSESSMENT

Understanding how to attract and select the very best candidates is critical to the success of the recruitment process. This assessment covers the key skills for effectively recruiting and selecting employees to sustain and develop your business.

Rate yourself on each of the techniques.
7 is competent and confident, little need for improvement
4 is average, needs improvement
1 is uncomfortable, major need for improvement

- Note specific areas of improvement related to each skill that you would like to develop. Be sure to include your *reasons* for your rating in each skill.
- Start thinking about a personal development plan and identify two or three things you could do to improve your skills in this area and write them in the space provided.

I…	Rating	Reasoning
approach the recruitment process as a strategic business activity and plan for employee turnover before I have a need.	1 2 3 4 5 6 7	
understand the high costs of recruitment and look for alternatives to fill employment vacancies.	1 2 3 4 5 6 7	
develop or review the job criteria (position description/candidate profile prior to undertaking a recruitment assignment.	1 2 3 4 5 6 7	
explore internal opportunities for filling employment vacancies prior to going external.	1 2 3 4 5 6 7	
tap into the external employee network by going beyond internet advertising.	1 2 3 4 5 6 7	
prepare thoroughly for every employment interview by reviewing candidate information, arranging an appropriate interview environment, developing appropriate questions etc.	1 2 3 4 5 6 7	
use critical incident based interview techniques to review past behavior and predict future behavior of candidates.	1 2 3 4 5 6 7	
use situational interviewing techniques to uncover how candidates would be likely to react or behave in given situation.	1 2 3 4 5 6 7	
ask STAR questions to probe Situation/Task, Action, and Results.	1 2 3 4 5 6 7	

ACTIVITY 1: CONTINUED

I...	Rating	Reasoning
avoid the use of leading and multiple questions in the interview process.	1 2 3 4 5 6 7	
allow candidates to do most of the talking in the interview and give candidates my full attention.	1 2 3 4 5 6 7	
take notes during the interview to ensure key points/candidate responses are recorded.	1 2 3 4 5 6 7	
prepare summary reports on all candidates that I interview.	1 2 3 4 5 6 7	
assess candidates against the requirements of the job and make selection decisions based on facts and not emotions.	1 2 3 4 5 6 7	
conduct reference checks on preferred candidates.	1 2 3 4 5 6 7	
respond in writing to all candidates who have been unsuccessful in the recruitment process.	1 2 3 4 5 6 7	

Personal development plan ideas:

1

2

Now update your Learning Journal (page 73)

THE NEED TO RECRUIT

PART 2

ESTABLISHING THE NEED TO RECRUIT

Each recruitment exercise is an opportunity to analyze the requirements of the job and the organization prior to sourcing additional staff. The recruitment strategy should be based on the consideration of a number of potential options around the position and should not be an automatic exercise to 'refill'. The need to fill an existing position or to create a new position should be reviewed in line with the specific needs of the business. The value added by a position should be considered before proceeding to recruit. Positions may be restructured, transferred, enlarged or removed depending on organizational needs, and economic and market fluctuations.

Job Redesign

An employment vacancy is a good opportunity to re-examine whether the position needs to be filled at all. It may be possible to modify aspects of the job such as job task, work-flow, reporting lines, physical location etc so that other positions within the team or organization are expanded or enriched to cover the requirements of the role. This is a particularly relevant strategy in tough economic times and for organizations in competitive markets where there is pressure to reduce overhead costs. The process of natural attrition is preferable to a redundancy situation for both the employee and the organization.

Succession Planning - Transfers and Promotions

When an employment vacancy arises, consideration should be given to internal transfers or promotions as an easy and inexpensive alternative to external or formal recruitment. This strategy has the additional advantage of motivating existing staff by demonstrating the opportunity for career advancement.

Job Sharing

Job sharing has become a popular alternative to full-time employment in recent decades with the increased number of women returning to the workforce after having children. These employees are critical members of the talent pool for many organizations and in a job-share arrangement can provide specialist skills on a part-time basis, while providing full-time coverage of the position. Prior to external recruitment taking place, the organization should consider members of the workforce due to return from maternity leave, or those considering staged retirement, as an alternative to re-hire.

Part-time Employment

Job vacancies should also be assessed against the potential for part-time replacement as opposed to full-time. This has the benefit of delivering a cost-saving to the organization, while providing more flexible work arrangements to interested employees. While some industries are more suited to the provision of part-time work, it is an opportunity that all organizations could consider by assessing the real full-time value and deliverables of the position.

Contract and Temporary Staff

Casual, contract and temporary staff may be a more flexible option than permanent or part-time replacement given that these employees can be hired for short-term and on-call work assignments. The advantage of casual employees includes flexibility and a reduction in fixed overhead costs. They are also a good interim measure while the longer-term needs of the position and the business are assessed. Temporary and contract employees can be recruited on a similar basis for the purpose of completing specific project work.

Executive Leasing

At senior levels it is possible to 'lease' executives for special assignments. Such executives can be obtained from specialist consultants or from a potential pool of retired or semi-retired employees.

Key considerations in establishing a recruitment need:

- What is the primary function of the position?
- How can the position be improved (for the organization and employee)?
- What type of person should be employed in the position?
- Can elements of the position be reallocated, modified, or eliminated entirely?
- Does the performance of the previous incumbent offer any lessons as the position's importance, effectiveness, or business impact?
- Can the position by filled internally via transfer or promotion?

Regardless of the alternatives available, when an employment vacancy arises, the recruiting manager must decide whether to fill the position via the normal recruitment and selection process, or to investigate one or more of the options outlined above. All of the above strategies have advantages and disadvantages. The decision whether to recruit or not will depend on the needs of the organization and the foresight of the recruiting manager and human resources department (where it exists) regarding long-term workforce planning. However, the costs involved in external recruitment should ensure that all other alternatives are considered first.

Complete Activity # 2
Terms & Definitions Match

ACTIVITY 2: TERMS & DEFINITIONS MATCH

Draw a line to match each term in the left column to the correct definition in the right column.

Term	Definition
Contract and Temporary Staff	Modification to aspects of the job such as job tasks, responsibilities, work-flow, reporting lines, physical location etc so that other positions within the team or organization are expanded or enriched to cover the requirements of the role.
Executive Leasing	Employment vacancies filled by internal transfers or promotions as an alternative to external or formal recruitment. This strategy motivates existing staff by demonstrating the opportunity for career advancement.
Job Redesign	Enabling two incumbents to provide specialist skills on a part-time basis, while providing full-time coverage to a position, is a strategy often used to accommodate employees returning from maternity leave, or those considering staged retirement.
Job Sharing	Delivers overhead cost-savings to the business while providing more flexible work arrangements to interested employees.
Part-time Employment	A more flexible option than permanent or part-time replacement given that these employees can be hired for short-term and on-call work assignments. The advantage of these employees includes flexibility and a reduction in fixed overhead costs. They are also a good interim measure while the longer-term needs of the position and the business are assessed.
Succession Planning	Use of executives for special assignments. Such executives can be obtained from specialist consultants or from a potential pool of retired or semi-retired employees.

Activity # 2 - Check your Answers

Check your work from the previous activity.

Terms	Definitions
Job Redesign	Modification to aspects of the job such as job tasks, responsibilities, work-flow, reporting lines, physical location etc so that other positions within the team or organization are expanded or enriched to cover the requirements of the role.
Succession Planning	Employment vacancies filled by internal transfers or promotions as an alternative to external or formal recruitment. This strategy motivates existing staff by demonstrating the opportunity for career advancement.
Job Sharing	Enabling two incumbents to provide specialist skills on a part-time basis, while providing full-time coverage to a position, is a strategy often used to accommodate employees returning from maternity leave, or those considering staged retirement.
Part-time Employment	Delivers overhead cost-savings to the business while providing more flexible work arrangements to interested employees.
Contract and Temporary Staff	A more flexible option than permanent or part-time replacement given that these employees can be hired for short-term and on-call work assignments. The advantage of these employees includes flexibility and a reduction in fixed overhead costs. They are also a good interim measure while the longer-term needs of the position and the business are assessed.
Executive Leasing	Use of executives for special assignments. Such executives can be obtained from specialist consultants or from a potential pool of retired or semi-retired employees.

Now update your Learning Journal (page 73)

DETERMINING THE REQUIREMENTS OF THE POSITION

Where the decision to recruit is made, the recruiting manager and or human resources (HR) department must develop or amend the Position Description and Candidate Profile. These documents are critical in driving the recruitment process, and heavily impacts the interview preparation and planning process.

Position Description

The Position Description details the work actually performed in the position including key tasks and responsibilities. It also sets out the nature of the relationship between a specific position and other positions within the organization, and outlines the position's expected contribution to the achievement of divisional or overall organizational goals.

The Position Description ensures that recruiting managers are clear about:

- The purpose of the position.
- Job responsibilities.
- Job dimensions.
- Reporting/functional relationships.
- Key competencies.

"Whether you're recruiting new employees or posting jobs for internal applicants, the job description tells the candidate exactly what you want in your selected person."

SUSAN M. HEATHFIELD

Tips for Developing Position Descriptions

- Position Descriptions should clearly communicate your company direction and where the employee fits in the big picture.
- Position Descriptions should set clear expectations for what you expect from people, and should be the first place you look if people aren't doing what you want them to do.
- Position Descriptions should cover any/all of your legal bases.
- Position Descriptions should help you select preferred candidates and address the issues and questions of candidates who were not selected.
- Position Descriptions should help existing employees work with and understand the expectations of new hires.
- Development of the position description is a good opportunity to involve existing employees in the recruitment process and get buy-in into the selection decision.

Candidate Profile

A Candidate Profile details the:

- skills (capacity to do something, ability to carry out relevant functions and tasks)
- knowledge (understanding of processes, issues & systems)
- attributes (personal habits and behaviors that support success)
- qualifications
- experience required for effective performance in the job, or which a person might reasonably be expected to have before appointment to a particular position.

Often, the Position Description and Candidate Profile are contained in the one document.

Conditions of Employment

Also important in determining the requirements of the position are identifying the conditions of employment. Employment Conditions, in addition to the Position Description and Candidate Profile, are important in establishing selection criteria when screening applicants. Considerations around employment conditions should be base on the following decisions:

- Is the position full-time, part-time, casual or contract?
- Is the position covered by a collective agreement or individual employment contract?
- Is the position weekly (hourly/weekly paid) or monthly paid (salaried staff)?
- What is the salary/wage review system for this position?
- Is the position covered by a formal job grade/salary band system?
- What are the other employment benefits/conditions attached to this position?
- What is the the necessary location and working arrangements for this position? E.g. Global or local; Office-based, remote or hybrid.

Recruiting Managers need to be clear on which employment category or arrangement a vacancy fits to ensure correct budgeting and reporting processes, and to ensure that any legal considerations are effectively covered. For example, an 'employee' has very different legal entitlements to 'casual' or 'contract' labour.

Position Description
+
Candidate Profile
+
Employment Conditions
=
Criteria for Attracting Candidates and
&
Criteria for Screening Candidates

POSITION DESCRIPTION
Completed Sample

Position Title:	Personal Assistant
Department/Unit:	Corporate Marketing
Responsible to:	Manager, Corporate Marketing
Directly Supervising:	Nil
Functional Relationships with:	Marketing Sales Consumer Services
Primary Objective:	To provide PA/ Secretarial support for Manager Corporate Marketing

Key Tasks	Expected Results	Control Information
Typing	▪ Copy typing using MS Word, PowerPoint & Excel ▪ Confidential correspondence & contracts	▪ All documents completed accurately and efficiently ▪ Confidentiality maintained
Organization	▪ Maintain appointment diaries ▪ Effectively and efficiently arrange events, meetings and conferences ▪ Arrange travel for Manager and other department team members	▪ Appointment diaries up to date ▪ All arrangements run smoothly and without incident
Administration	▪ Ensure mail distributed/ actioned in a timely manner ▪ Stationery available as required ▪ Accounts up to date	▪ Administration up to date and in order
Budgeting	▪ Assist with preparation and maintenance of cost centre and corporate budgets	▪ Budgets prepared accurately and on time ▪ Changes maintained as necessary
Filing	▪ Update and maintain files for Manager and team	▪ Files up to date
Support	▪ Participate in projects as directed ▪ Take minutes in meetings and action relevant tasks in a timely and efficient manner	▪ Projects completed on time and to standard

ACTIVITY 3A: CREATE A POSITION DESCRIPTION

Download the **TPC Position Description** from https://www.catherinematttiske.com/books

Activity using the TPC Position Description tool:

1 - Make sure you have downloaded the TPC Position Description

2 - Review the sample TPC Position Description on Page 24.

3 - Using the TPC Position Description, create a position description for a real life role. If you do not require a new position description for one of your team, or don't have a team, create a position description for your own role.

Now update your Learning Journal (page 73)

CANDIDATE PROFILE
Completed Sample

Job Title: Personal Assistant - Corporate Marketing
Reporting To: Chris Johnson

Education

Essential	Desirable
High School Certificate or equivalent	Business College or formal Office Administration training
	University or College Degree

Experience

Essential	Desirable
Minimum 3 years secretarial, or personal assistant experience in a medium or large company	Marketing experience
	Working in the Pharmaceutical Industry
	Customer Service Experience

Knowledge & Skills

Essential	Desirable
Skills:	
Microsoft Word	Fluent in Spanish and/or German
Strong Verbal Communication	Microsoft Excel
Excellent Written Communication	Microsoft PowerPoint
Accuracy & attention to detail	Adobe Acrobat
Microsoft Outlook	
Keyboard Skills - 80 wpm, 99% accuracy	
Knowledge:	
Marketing Fundamentals	

Personal Qualities

Essential	Desirable
Co-operative	
Professional	
Confidential	
Uses Initiative	

Values

Essential	Desirable
Fast paced	Customer Service
Organized	Innovative
Team Player	Creative
Positive	Collaboration
Respectful	Sense of Community

ACTIVITY 3B: CANDIDATE PROFILE

 Download the **TPC Candidate Profile** from https://www.catherinematttiske.com/books

Activity using the TPC Candidate Profile tool:

Refer to the Position Description that you created in Activity 3A, and now:

1 - Downloaded the TPC Candidate Profile

2 - Review the sample TPC Candidate Profile on Page 26.

3 - Use the TPC Candidate Profile tool to create a candidate profile for a real life role.

Remember, if you do not require a new candidate profile for one of your team, or don't have a team, create a candidate profile for your own role.

Now update your Learning Journal (page 73)

"
"When I meet successful people I ask 100 questions as to what they attribute their success to. It is usually the same: persistence, hard work and hiring good people."

KIANA TOM

SOURCING EMPLOYEES

PART 3

INTERNAL SOURCES OF EMPLOYEES

"You can employ men and hire hands to work for you, but you must win their hearts to have them work with you."

RIORIO

Recruiting managers together with Human Resources will determine the best recruitment strategy for filling a position. A vacancy may be filled internally in several ways.

1. Direct appointment or promotion by management

The advantage of this strategy is a quick decision allowing management to demonstrate an internal reward system, or the succession planning process at work. While this approach has the benefit of motivating promoted employees, it could be open to abuse, and managers may be accused of favoritism unless the appointment is clearly the result of a visible succession plan or some other fair selection process.

2. Lateral transfer of an employee from one team or department to another

This strategy can be used when the vacancy presents an opportunity to develop another employee's skills on the same level. Employees may be keen to accept a sideways move where there is perceived benefit in picking up new tasks and responsibilities, and broader

exposure to other parts of the business. This can provide incentive to employees who are keen to grow their skills in the interests of longer term career development.

3. Internal Advertising

This strategy widens the pool of potential candidates and helps identify talented and interested employees who may otherwise be overlooked in formal succession planning activities. This method has the added advantage of boosting employee satisfaction and morale by communicating that the organization is committed to providing career development opportunities and long term employment for its people. For these reasons, many organizations have a policy to advertise all employment vacancies internally, and only resort to external appointments when the internal talent pool has been exhausted.

Advantages of Internal Advertising

- Helps employees manager their own careers by applying for positions rather than being pushed into identified roles by management.

- Existing employees can be more easily appraised or assessed against the requirements of the position than external employees. Errors in the selection process are therefore less likely to occur.

- Simplifies the recruitment process by focusing on internal succession planning and limiting external recruitment to lower-level positions which serve as an 'entry-point' to the organization.

- Is a much more cost effective method than external advertising or the use of recruitment agencies.

Disadvantages of Internal Advertising

- May attract applications from employees who are unsuitable and unqualified for the position, even though they may be good performers in their current role. The challenge for the organization is to keep employees motivated in the current role so that they continue to make a positive contribution, and develop them for future opportunities.

- Advising internal applicants that they have been unsuccessful needs to be treated more sensitively than with external candidates. These employees need to walk away from the recruitment process with their pride in tact, and their morale high.

- A series of unsuccessful applications may be regarded by the employee as direct criticism of their work performance and contribution, with adverse affects on their motivation and morale.

- An application by an internal candidate may be perceived by the candidates manager as a criticism of the manager's performance, particularly if the application is for a lateral move.

The Decision not to Advertise Internally

Organizations may decide to omit internal advertising and make a direct appointment where:

- A reorganization has occurred.
- An employee is returning from a transfer or assignment and is appropriate for the position.
- A successor has been specifically prepared to fill the position.
- The position represents a special assignment.
- There is a direct exchange of employees for experience.

SAMPLE
INTERNAL ADVERTISEMENT

Post Notice to: Head Office
Regional Sales Offices
State Manufacturing Sites

Inventory Controller

The ABC Widget's Factory located in X currently has a vacancy for an Inventory Controller.

Reporting to the Resources Manager, this important position is responsible for ongoing inventory accuracy, coordination and preparation of impact studies, and working closely with both shop floor and management to continuously improve inventory systems and procedures.

The position would suit someone who has or is currently studying towards CPIM qualifications, or who has previous BPCS and MRPII experience in a factory environment.

Applicants should be able to demonstrate a high degree of initiative, with accuracy and attention to detail. Good verbal and written communication skills are also essential.

If you are interested in pursuing this challenging opportunity and have the necessary attributes as outlined, please forward your application (including a current C.V.) to:

XYZ
xyzhr@abclimited.com
Human Resources Advisor
ABC Limited
PO Box 000
WIDGET TOWN

Applications close DATE

EXTERNAL SOURCES OF EMPLOYEES

Where attempts to fill the vacancy internally have failed, recruiting managers and HR will agree on the best strategy for attracting external candidates. If the list of potential internal candidates is reviewed and there are no suitable employees, the organization should seek to fill the position externally.

This is also an appropriate strategy if a decision has been made to attract "fresh talent" for the purpose of bringing in new skills and behaviors. Whatever the organization does, it should be consistent in its approach i.e., employees should be fully aware of the policies and procedures around the internal versus external recruitment process and under which circumstance each will be used.

There are a variety of media and strategies through which a potential talent pool can be reached. While the primary sources are internet advertising and online media, there are several other methods for attracting external candidates.

1. Tap Employee Networks

- Spread word-of-mouth information about position availability, or eventual availability, to employees so they can tune into potential candidates in their networks of friends and colleagues.

- Take advantage of your industry contacts, association memberships and trade groups.

- Pay for employees to participate in network and in industry groups.

- Use extensive telephone and online networking. Bring people in for interviews before you have an available position.

2. Use the Website for Recruiting

- Use your company website and online media to tell and even, "sell," potential employees about the vision, mission, values and culture of your company.

- Your website needs to set your company apart from others in your industry. Your job listings must motivate a potential candidate to think, "this organization is for me!" The website should also provide a way for candidates to easily submit resumes for consideration for future positions.

- Follow-up all website and online submissions with a greeting that thanks the individual for their interest in your company. Send a periodic update about your job openings. Your professional, ongoing contact with interested people ensures recruiting success.

3. Become an Employer of Choice

- Think about what a potential employee considers before agreeing to join your organization or business. Are you stable, making money and growing? Are you employee-friendly? Does your mission appeal to the mind-set of the people you most want to recruit? Will your organization provide exciting opportunities for challenge and professional growth?

- Analyze every component of your recruiting process to make sure that you are sending these messages. If you want to be an employer of choice, you must act like an employer of choice. Further more, you must communicate this commitment to your prospective employees.

- Being an employer of choice is a reputation you build in your industry that is a powerful tool in attracting top talent.

"If you hire mediocre people, they will hire mediocre people."

TOM MURPHY,
AMERICAN BUSINESSMAN,
CEO OF CAPITAL CITIES, ABC

4. Recruit Using the Internet

- Post your positions on professional association or industry websites and online networks, online employment or job search services sites to cast your net as wide as possible. Research indicates that job seeker's begin their search and most often use this method to investigate job opportunities.

- Post the ad on professional online networks such as LinkedIn. Many potential applicants have their profiles already created on these networks, which makes it easier for them to apply in a few clicks for the advertised position.

- Make sure your recruitment ads 'sell' the vision and the advantages of your organization. Effective ads portray your company as an exciting and rewarding place to work.

5. Use 'Headhunters' and Recruiters

- Sometimes, it is worth your time to use 'headhunters', recruiters and employment placement firms. The best firms have done much of this homework and candidate pool development for you.

- For some positions and in some industries, the cost of your time and the time invested in a possible failed search, are worth it.

- Additionally, as recruiters have an already-developed pool of candidates, they may provide a second pair of experienced eyes to help you with your search, and they can quickly organize a shortlist of suitable, interested candidates.

6. Use Temporary Agencies and Firms for the Recruitment of Non-Specialized Staff

- Consider using temporary staff as a solution to 'try a person out in a position' or to staff a position you are not sure you need for the long term.

- Temporary employees can provide a useful buffer for the ups and downs of the business cycle so that you do not have to affect your core staff during down times.

- Temp firms will recruit and screen to your specifications and guarantee your satisfaction. They save your staff immense amounts of time as they provide testing, drug screening, reference checking, background checks, and anything else you'd like, for a nominal fee.

- Additionally, as the firms become familiar with your needs, just as 'headhunters' and recruiters do, they will seek out and suggest talent they believe meets your criteria for star candidates.

7. Take Advantage of Positive Publicity

- The publicity your organization receives in the news media, in print, on television, on the radio and online is critical for recruiting.

- A few good words, an interesting article or a piece about your mission that reflects your organization in a favorable light, will result in candidates coming to you. And that, in my way of thinking, is the best way of all to find great candidates for your candidate pool.

External Advertising Summary

All recruitment advertising, even a small ad, should be planned on the basis of four questions.

- What do you want to accomplish?
    - What are the recruitment goals?
    - What is the role of advertising in achieving them?
- Who are the people you want to reach?
    - Who are the likely applicants?
    - What are their characteristics and motivations?
- What is the appropriate advertising message?
    - What information about the job and the organization will persuade suitably qualified people to apply?
- How should the message be presented?
    - What media should be used?

Successful recruitment advertising does not necessarily bring a large volume of applications, however, should attract high calibre applicants.

An effective advertisement will:

- Outline what the job is - describe main roles and responsibilities.
- Attract the interest of potential applicants.
- Be clear and concise.
- Encourage applicants to respond because they view the advertised position as an improvement on their present situation.

Complete Activity # 4a
Internal Recruitment Advertising

Complete Activity # 4b
Growing the External Talent Pool

ACTIVITY 4A: INTERNAL RECRUITMENT ADVERTISING

For the same position you developed the Position Description / Candidate Profile for in Activity # 3, prepare an internal job vacancy to advertise this position.

INTERNAL VACANCY

Now update your Learning Journal (page 73)

ACTIVITY 4B: GROWING THE EXTERNAL TALENT POOL

Consider your top three strategies for attracting external candidates and describe how you could implement these to grow your potential talent pool.

Strategies for Attracting External Candidates	How I could implement this strategy to grow my potential talent pool?
1.	
2.	
3.	

Now update your Learning Journal (page 73)

THE INTERVIEWING PROCESS

PART 4

THE INTERVIEW PROCESS

The job interview is a universal tool of the recruitment process and is possibly the most important part of selecting a suitable candidate. During the interview, interviewers have the responsibility of representing and promoting the organization to candidates, gathering information from candidates; and assessing candidate suitability for the position.

Interview Preparation

The success of any interview depends largely on the amount of preparation you do before you come face-to-face with the candidate. You need to ensure that appropriate arrangements are in place for scheduling and conducting interviews. Candidates should be contacted and informed of the date, time, place, and who to ask for prior the interview date. Where possible, reception should also be briefed as to who is arriving at what time.

It is important to ensure that a suitable room has been booked to conduct the interview, and that you are free from other work and possible interruptions for the duration of the interview. Care and attention must also be given to the physical setting of the interview to ensure adequate light, heating, cooling, ventilation and an environment free from noise and distraction. Seating should be comfortable, and interviewers and candidates should not be divided by a desk. Where practical, a small round table is more suitable.

If interviewing via virtual meeting, similar consideration should be given to the environment in which the virtual interview will be conducted.

Interview structure and questions should also be prepared in advance. This means re-familiarizing yourself with the requirements of the position and determining the best approach for assessing candidates against this criteria. How detailed and standardised your interview guide is, will depend on the volume of recruitment that you do, how frequently a particular vacancy occurs, and how involved you are in the process.

It is critical, prior to interview that you know as much about the candidate as possible. This will avoid wasting time asking questions that are already covered in the application, and helps to establish rapport with candidates by showing that you have done your research and are interested in them.

"We often say that the biggest job we have is to teach a newly hired employee to fail intelligently... to experiment over and over again and to keep on trying and failing until he learns what will work."

CHARLES F. KETTERING 1876-1958, AMERICAN ENGINEER, INVENTOR

Conducting the Interview

An interview has three key stages:

1. Opening

A successful 'open' should introduce the people present at the interview and their purpose for being there, provide an outline of how the interview will run, and encourage candidates to relax. First impressions are critical on both sides and the ability to establish rapport quickly puts everybody at ease.

2. Information Exchange

During this stage, interviewers communicate information about the position, explore candidate background and experience, and ask relevant questions in relation to the applicant's work history and skills. The candidate also has an opportunity to present information about themselves, relate their skills and experiences to the position, and ask questions specific to the job role and the organization. With the applicant's permission, notes should be taken by the interviewer during this stage.

3. Close

The close is the formal 'wrap-up' of the interview. During this stage the interviewer should be very clear about the next steps in the recruitment process, and when the applicant is likely to hear back from the organization, whether they have been successful or not. Candidates should leave the interview with clear expectations about when they will receive some feedback. The interviewer should also make certain that the applicant is still interested in the position at this point.

Types of Interviews

There are two common interview styles which have been tried and tested to select the best candidates.

1. Critical Incident Based Interviews

Critical incident based interviewing works on the principle that "past performance is the best predictor of future performance." Using this strategy, the goal of the interview is to probe examples of past behavior that can be applied to future behavior, and that are relevant to the position. All interview questions focus on the candidate's past experience and are designed to formulate a behavioral profile.

Typically questions are constructed around:

- A specific situation that the candidate faced.
- The candidate's behavior in that situation.
- The outcome of the candidate's behavior.

Questions should target key competencies for the position. Generally the interviewer will select 4-6 of the most relevant competencies for the position and interview in detail for about 15 minutes each.

2. Situational Interviewing

Is similar to the Behavioral Interview, except that candidates are asked what they would do (not what they have done) in a particular situation. For both styles of interviewing, questions should be prepared based on the STAR model...

S / T	What was the **S**ituation or **T**ask?
A	What **A**ction was taken (the Behavior)?
R	What was the **R**esult (the Outcome)?

Sample STAR Questions

S / T	Describe a difficult problem that you have had to deal with?
A	How did you deal with this situation?
R	What happened in this situation and how would you handle it now in retrospect?

S / T	What type of things put you under pressure? Please give me an example.
A	How did you cope with this situation?
R	What happened in this situation?

S / T	Describe a situation when you've had to choose between two different courses of action.
A	How did you make your decision?
R	What happened and how did you evaluate whether you had made the right decision?

More on Questioning

1. Open Questions

This type of question encourages the candidate to talk, and provide information in their own words. These questions typically start with Who, What, When, Why, How or Where.

For example:

- How do you think you applied your knowledge and experience to your work?
- What particular strengths and knowledge do you think you've developed this year?

Open questions are effective in helping to establish rapport and to explore opinions, attitudes and feelings.

2. Probing Questions

This type of question helps to get under the surface of an initial response by encouraging deeper feelings or broader responses. For example, having asked an open question such as:

- What was the organization's comment on your actions? The interviewer could follow up with a probing question.
- How did you handle their response?

Probing questions are particularly useful for encouraging people to concentrate on specific points, for clarifying uncertainties, testing the validity of a more general response and seeking contrary evidence.

3. Closed Questions

This type of question requires short or yes/no answers. For example,

- Do you enjoy working as part of a multi-disciplinary team?

The effect of a closed question is to close down a conversation. Closed questions can be used to obtain or check specific, concise information. However, they are not appropriate if you are trying to get the interviewee to talk in depth about their feelings or their experience.

4. Leading Questions

This type of question facilitates the expected answer. For example,

- Don't you think that strong discipline is the solution?

Leading questions tend to reveal more about the interviewer than the interviewee, as their effect is to encourage or possibly compel the interviewee to say what the interviewer wants to hear, rather than what they actually think. They are usually based on assumptions on the part of the interviewer and should be avoided.

5. Multiple Questions

This type of question has several parts or questions in one. The interviewer asks a string of questions without pausing to allow the interviewee to reply. For example.

- How does your current job compare with your last one, which aspect presented greatest difficulty, and how difficult did you find it to keep up-to-date?

Multiple questions confuse the interviewee as they don't know which part of them to answer. These questions should be broken down so that the interviewee can answer each independently.

Library of Interview Questions

Questions about Work History

1. Start: Questions about name of company, position title and description, dates of employment.
2. What were your expectations for the job and to what extent were they met?
3. What were your starting and final levels of compensation?
4. What were your responsibilities?
5. What major challenges and problems did you face? How did you handle them?
6. Which was most / least rewarding?
7. What was the biggest accomplishment / failure in this position?
8. Questions about your supervisors and co-workers.
9. What was it like working for your supervisor? What were his/her strengths and shortcomings?
10. Who was your best boss and who was the worst?
11. Why are you looking for a new opportunity?
12. What have you been doing since your last job?

Questions about the Candidate

1. What is your greatest weakness?
2. What is your greatest strength?
3. Describe a typical work week.
4. Do you take work home with you?
5. How many hours do you normally work?
6. How would you describe the pace at which you work?
7. How do you handle stress and pressure?
8. What motivates you?
9. What are your salary expectations?
10. What do you find are the most difficult decisions to make?
11. Tell me about yourself.
12. What has been the greatest disappointment in your life?
13. What frustrates you?
14. What do people most often criticize about you?
15. When was the last time you were angry? What happened?
16. If you could relive the last 10 years of your life, what would you do differently?
17. If the people who know you were asked why you should be hired, what would they say?
18. Do you prefer to work independently or on a team?

19. Give some examples of teamwork.
20. What type of work environment do you prefer?
21. How do you evaluate success?
22. If you know your boss is 100% wrong about something how would you handle it?
23. Describe a difficult work situation / project and how you overcame it.
24. Describe a time when your workload was heavy and how you handled it.
25. More job interview questions about your abilities.
26. More job interview questions about you.

Questions About The Future

1. What are you looking for in your next job? What is important to you?
2. What are your goals for the next five years / ten years?
3. How do you plan to achieve those goals?
4. What are your salary requirements - both short-term and long-term?
5. Questions about your career goals.
6. What will you do if you don't get this position?

Questions About the New Job and the Company

1. What interests you about this job?
2. Why do you want this job?
3. What applicable attributes / experience do you have?
4. Are you overqualified for this job?
5. What can you do for this company?
6. Why should we hire you?
7. Why are you the best person for the job?
8. What do you know about this company?
9. Why do you want to work here?
10. What challenges are you looking for in a position?
11. What can you contribute to this company?
12. Are you willing to travel?
13. Is there anything I haven't told you about the job or company that you would like to know?

Library of Target Based and Sales Interview Questions

Target Based and Sales Interviews are often the most difficult for recruiting managers. The following questions are designed to assist when recruiting these professionals.

General Questions

1. Why did you go into the sales profession?
2. Why do you enjoy selling?
3. What is it you like about sales?
4. Where do you want sales to lead you in your career?
5. Tell me about the accomplishments you are most proud of.
6. Describe to me the details of your last three days at work.
7. What do you like and dislike about the products or services you're selling now and why?
8. What attracts you to the industry you are in?
9. What are your long-term professional goals?
10. What do you do personally for your professional development?
11. What are your favorite selling books?
12. As a sales professional, what do you see as your primary and secondary roles within a company?
13. Describe a time where a creative approach to meeting an objective didn't work and what you did next.
14. What is the largest group you've presented to (externally/ internally)?
15. What do you like and dislike about presentations and why?
16. Describe a time you led a group of people, the primary challenges you faced and how you handled them.
17. What would you say your one or two biggest failures or mistakes were? What did you learn from them?
18. What are some of the challenges you see that are facing this industry?
19. How would those with whom you work now, across all areas of the company, describe you and the work you do?
20. Are you an individual contributor or do you sell as part of a sales team?
21. Tell me about the product you sold in your last job.
22. What kinds of rewards do you find most satisfying?
23. How do you keep yourself going when everyone around you is complaining about having a bad day?
24. Do you meet report deadlines?
25. What lead sources have you found most productive?
26. Does your company provide you with leads?

Sales Skills Questions

1. Why do you think people buy from you?
2. What are the top two or three most important sales skills one should possess? Why?
3. Tell me about your two most satisfying sales deals and why they were your best.
4. Tell me about two deals you've lost. Why did you lose them? Who was the competitor you lost them to? What did you learn from losing them?
5. How do you deal with rejection?
6. What areas would your two most recent Managers say you should improve upon to become stronger?
7. Describe a situation with a client or prospect where you could have taken a different approach. What would you have done differently?
8. Describe a couple of instances, big or small, where you took a different approach in achieving an objective outside the company direction?
9. How do you organize a presentation?
10. What do you think are the most important skills in succeeding in sales?
11. What are your top three open-ended questions for initial sales calls?
12. In your current sales environment, describe the process you go through to qualify your prospects?
13. What is your biggest difficulty in selling?
14. Tell me about a recent sale that you lost to a competitor.
15. Give me an example of a recent difficult sale and how you closed the deal.

Sales Cycle/Process Questions

1. What's the average length of a sales cycle?
2. Describe your typical sales cycle.
3. What do you feel are the two most important things you need from a company to get off on the right track?
4. What do you like and dislike about the sales process and why?
5. What type of sales cycle is most rewarding to you? A long cycle for a big-ticket item or a series of smaller, more frequent sales.

'Typical Week' Questions

1. How many first appointments do you have each week?
2. How many rejections do you take in a typical week?
3. In your current position, how much time would you say you spend directly with prospects and customers throughout the sales day?
4. What do you see as the key issues in negotiating?
5. How would your present prospects and customers describe you as their sales representative?
6. Does your company support the sales force?
7. Describe a time your company did not deliver on its product or service and how you responded.
8. How strong is your pipeline?
9. Describe how you present a solution to your prospective client?
10. At what stage in the sales process do you present the ROI to the prospect?
11. Describe one or two of the most difficult challenges and/ or rejections you've faced in the past and how you responded?

Quota Questions

1. Over the past three years, what percentage of your quota did you achieve?
2. Have you ever worked in a commission only job?
3. How were you rated in your last three performance reviews?

Closing Questions

1. Tell me about a time when you were in a "closing situation" and for whatever reason, the "decision-maker" couldn't make a decision. What did you do? Did you get the deal?
2. What do you see as the key skills in closing?

Complete Activity # 5
Developing Interview Questions

© 2022, TPC - The Performance Company Pty Limited. All rights reserved.

ACTIVITY 5: DEVELOPING INTERVIEW QUESTIONS

Based on the Position Description, Candidate Profile, and Internal Recruitment Advertisement you prepared in the previous activities, develop appropriate questions that you would ask a potential candidate in interviewing for this position.

Now update your Learning Journal (page 73)

THE IMPORTANCE OF LISTENING IN INTERVIEWS

- Allow the applicant to do most of the talking - the ratio should be around 80/20.
- Give the applicant your full attention and do not allow them to gloss over important details.
- Listening is a good opportunity to assess the applicants communication, speech and vocabulary skills.
- Pause to persuade the applicant to elaborate or continue on a particular issue.
- Clues for further questions may result from answers that the applicant gives. For example, if the applicant mentions undertaking a course of study, it would be wise to ask whether this was successfully completed or passed.
- Listening enables careful evaluation of words. For example, if an applicant claims to have held a managerial position, the interviewer should determine exactly what this implied in terms of duties and responsibilities.
- We think more quickly than we talk so listen carefully to hear what the applicant actually says rather than allowing your mind to run ahead to assumptions.
- Check for understanding by restating what has just been said using your own words. This can be done at an appropriate time - usually when the applicant pauses for a reaction.
- Listen not only to the words but also to the way they are said and to the feelings behind the words. This leads to a clearer and deeper understanding of what the applicant is actually trying to say.

Note Taking

Permission to take notes should be obtained from the applicant at the start of the interview. Note taking should be ongoing throughout the interview process, however should also be discreet. If every word is recorded, candidates may begin to feel uncomfortable and modify their answers accordingly. Too much attention on note taking also reduces the level of rapport with candidates.

After the Interview

After the interview, a full report should be prepared as soon as possible while the interviewer's memory is still fresh. If this is left too late, there will be a tendency to 'fill in the gaps', resulting in less reliable information. This is particularly important if several applicants are being interviewed on the same day. The interview report should contain all the necessary identification data and should be based on the selection criteria. Notes made during the interview should also be attached.

"Never hire someone who knows less than you do about what he's hired to do."

MALCOLM S. FORBES

Complete Activity # 6
Interview Report Form

ACTIVITY 6: INTERVIEW REPORT FORM

 Download the **TPC Interview Report Form** from https://www.catherinematttiske.com/books

 **Activity using the TPC Interview Report Form**

- Carefully review the tool
- Modify or amend the tool for your organizational needs

Now update your Learning Journal (page 73)

"Surround yourself with the best people you can find, delegate authority, and don't interfere as long as the policy you've decided upon is being carried out."

RONALD REAGAN

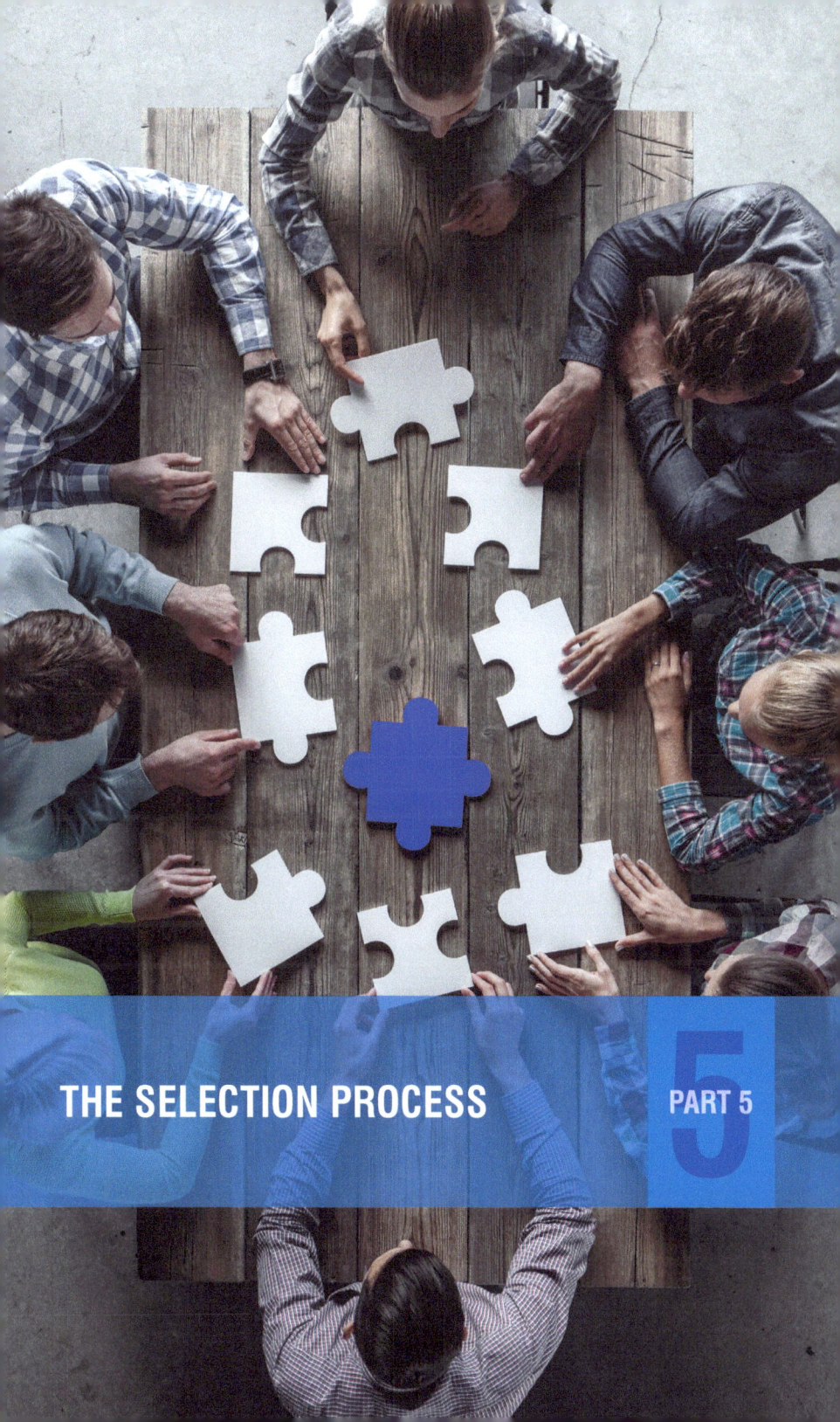

THE SELECTION PROCESS

PART 5

THE SELECTION DECISION

"It's easy to make good decisions when there are no bad options."

ROBERT HALF

Ultimately, the purpose of all recruitment activity and gathering of candidate information is to enable the organization to make a well-informed selection decision. However, actually selecting the best candidate is probably one of the most difficult aspects of the recruitment process.

Before a final decision is made, recruiting managers should review the position description and candidate profile for the position. This ensures that candidates are appointed according to suitability for the position and the decision is based on facts rather than emotions.

The selection decision should involve ranking short-listed candidates against parameters of the position description and candidate profile. The process should be as systematic as possible, especially where there are large amounts of data about a number of different candidates. Careful examination of the facts will help to focus on the job related criteria.

For some management or executive positions a second interview may be needed and if necessary request potential candidates complete psychrometric testing.

Complete Activity # 7
Candidate Assessment Summary

ACTIVITY 7: CANDIDATE ASSESSMENT SUMMARY

 Download the **TPC Candidate Assessment Summary** from https://www.catherinematttiske.com/books

Activity using the TPC Candidate Assessment Summary

- Carefully review the tool
- Modify or amend the tool for your organizational needs

Now update your Learning Journal (page 73)

Reference Checking

Reference checks are an important part of the selection process, establishing the truth of applicant data and confirming impressions obtained during the interview process. Reference checks (normally conducted via phone) gather relevant applicant data from people with whom the applicant as previously been closely associated. Reference checks may be conducted on one or more preferred candidates, and should be carried out by the recruiting manager or Human Resources.

The most relevant information will come from the applicant's previous managers or supervisors. In cases where applicants are unwilling for contact to be made with an immediate manager, the reasons should be discussed with the applicant. If inability to contact a referee would prejudice an application, this should be pointed out to the applicant.

Interviewers can assist referee honesty by using a standard format, reassuring referees of confidentiality and enabling referees to focus on crucial job-related issues.

The Job Offer

Where an organization has a human resources department, HR generally makes the offer of employment. This ensures consistency across the organization, and ensures that procedures for observing wage structures, salary rates, job gradings etc are maintained.

The initial job offer is usually verbal to save time and delay, and secure the selected candidate. A written offer should follow and should state the position, wages or salary, the start date, and any other relevant conditions of employment. While a written offer is the basis of the employee's employment contract, it is also an opportunity to market the organization and reassure successful candidates that they have made the right employment decision.

Advising Unsuccessful Applicants

An often overlooked aspect of the recruitment process is the need to advise unsuccessful applicants in a tactful and courteous manner. It is a basic courtesy to advise candidates of the outcome of their application, and even more important to have them continue to like you and your organization in the process.

It is relatively common for unsuccessful candidates to publicly complain of replies which are belated, abrupt, or even non-existent. The indirect consequences of a poor notification process are unsuccessful applicants spreading bad publicity about the company, refusing to use the products or services of the company, and encouraging others not to use the products or services of the company.

Many organizations use a standard approach to notify unsuccessful applicants. The content of such communication should include the following:

- A personal greeting.
- Appreciation of the candidates interest in working for the organization.
- Indication that the candidate was seriously considered for the position.
- Broad statement about the quality of the applications received.
- Statement advising that the candidate was unsuccessful.
- Good wishes for the future.

"When hiring key employees, there are only two qualities to look for: judgement and taste. Almost everything else can be bought by the yard."

JOHN W. GARDNER

TIPS AND TRAPS

PART 6

EIGHT HIRING MISTAKES EMPLOYERS MAKE: FROM APPLICATION TO INTERVIEW

Recruitment decisions that result in "bad" hires sap your organization's time, training resources, and energy. Following are eight mistakes to avoid during the recruiting and selection process.

1. Failure to Pre-screen Candidates

A half hour phone or virtual call can save hours of time. By pre-screening applicants you can uncover whether candidates have the knowledge and experience you need, and their salary expectations.

2. Failure to Prepare the Candidate

Prepare your candidates better for the interview by describing the company, details of the position, background and titles of the interviewers etc before they come in, so interviewers spend their time on the important issues: determining the candidate's skills and fit within your culture.

3. Failure to Prepare the Interviewers

Interviewers need to meet in advance and create an interview plan. Who is responsible for which questions? What aspect of the candidate's credentials is each person assessing? Who is assessing cultural fit etc?

---

[1] Susan M. Heathfield. Eight Hiring Mistakes Employers Make: From Application to Interview

4. Relying on the Interview to Evaluate a Candidate

During an interview, candidates tell you what they think you want to hear because they want to successfully obtain a job offer.

"The typical interview increases the likelihood of choosing the best candidate by less than 2%. In other words, if you just 'flipped' a coin you would be correct 50% of the time. If you added an interview you would only be right 52% of the time." Chally Group

Smart employers develop other methods for evaluating candidates in addition to the interview.

5. Failure to do Nothing But Talk During the Interview

Every interview needs to have components other than questions, answers and discussion. Where possible/if relevant, look for opportunities to observe the candidate perform a task, present back information, or problem-solve a case study etc. As long as you use tests and tasks that are directly related to the position, you will gain valuable insight into candidate suitability for the role.

6. Evaluate "Personality," Not Job Skills and Experience

People tend to hire people who are similar to themselves. This will kill your organization over time. You need diverse people with diverse personalities to deal with diverse employees, customers and situations. Hiring a candidate because you like them, ignores the need for particular skills and experience.

7. Failure to rank Candidates based on Critical Job Skills

How do you differentiate one candidate from another? You must decide on, and test, the skills you most desire in your candidate. Once you have established the critical success factors for the position, each candidate must be rated against these. You cannot afford to "settle" for a candidate that does not present the full complement of essential skills.

8. Failure to Develop a Solid Candidate Pool

Take the time to build a candidate pool with several candidates who meet the needs of your organization. If you don't have to make a choice among several qualified candidates, your pool is too small. Don't "settle" for someone if you don't have the right person with the skills and experience you need. It's better to reopen your search.

Complete Activity # 8
From Hiring Mistakes to Hiring Greats

ACTIVITY 8: FROM HIRING MISTAKES TO HIRING GREATS

For each of the Hiring Mistakes listed below, describe how you could turn this mistake into a strategy for hiring great candidates.

Hiring Mistake	How could I turn this into a strategy for hiring great candidates?
1. Failure to Pre-screen Candidates	
2. Failure to Prepare the Candidate	
3. Failure to Prepare the Interviewers	
4. Relying on the Interview to Evaluate a Candidate	
5. Failure to do Nothing But Talk During the Interview	
6. Evaluate "Personality," Not Job Skills and Experience	
7. Failure to rank Candidates based on Critical Job Skills	
8. Failure to Develop a Solid Candidate Pool	

Now update your Learning Journal (page 73)

"

"I believe the real difference between success and failure in a corporation can be very often traced to the question of how well the organization brings out the great energies and talents of its people."

THOMAS J. WATSON, JR.
A BUSINESS AND ITS BELIEFS (1963)

Section 2
LEARNING JOURNAL

The Learning Journal is used throughout the process to record your key learnings, hot tips and things to remember.

Update your Learning Journal at anytime. Ensure you complete your Learning Journal after you finish each activity. Then turn back to the Learning Short-take® to continue your learning.

LEARNING JOURNAL

As you work through this Learning Short-take®, make detailed notes on this page of the lessons you have learned and any useful skill areas. For each lesson or refresher point think about how you could further develop this skill. Your coach will want to discuss these with you in your Skill Development Action Planning meeting.

> "…that is what learning is.
> You suddenly understand something you've understood all your life, but in a new way."
> DORIS LESSING

> "Act as though it were impossible to fail."
> WINSTON CHURCHILL

"The wise do at once what the fool does later."
BALTASAR GRACIAN (1601-58), SPANISH JESUIT PRIEST AND AUTHOR.

Learning or Idea	Action to be taken	Result Expected

Learning Journal - continued

Learning or Idea	Action to be taken	Result Expected

"Anyone who stops learning is old, whether at twenty or eighty."
HENRY FORD

Learning or Idea	Action to be taken	Result Expected

"If you pick the right people and give them the opportunity to spread their wings - and put compensation as a carrier behind it - you almost don't have to manage them."

JACK WELCH

Section 3

SKILL DEVELOPMENT ACTION PLAN

Your Skill Development Action Plan is the last Step in the process. After you have completed the Learning Short-take® and all Activities, update your Learning Journal, then complete this section.

SKILL DEVELOPMENT ACTION PLAN

This is the most important part of the program - your individual Skill Development Action Plan.

You need to complete this plan before meeting with your manager or prior to on-going coaching. You will discuss it in detail with your manager or coach as he or she will ensure that you have everything you need to complete the tasks and activities.

Once you have completed your **Skill Development Action Plan** schedule a meeting time with your manager or coach to review your plan. Take your Learning Short-take® and all other documentation received during the training course to this meeting.

Remember - you have committed to your **Skill Development Action Plan**, and need to make time to complete your tasks!

"The mind, once stretched by a new idea, never regains its original dimensions."

OLIVER WENDELL HOLMES

"Whatever you can do or dream you can - begin it. Boldness has genius, power and magic."

JOHANN WOLFGANG VON GOETHE

"Imagination is the eye of the soul."
JOSEPH JOUBERT (1754-1824)

Task or activity (Be specific)	Measure (this will help you to know you have achieved it)	Date (Be specific)
Reflect on your Learning Journal. Transfer action items that you can apply to your job. Ensure that you include some 'stretch goals' and also a blend of short, medium and long term goals.	Apart from you, who else is needed to assist you in achieving your goal.	Be specific. A general date such as 'Quarter 1', 'August', or 'by end of year' is vague and more likely to result in not achieving your target. Be specific – e.g. 22nd November.

IDEAS FOR DISCUSSION WITH MY MANAGER

Ideas

CONGRATULATIONS!

You've now completed this Learning Short-take®.

Meet with your Manager/Coach to discuss your Skill Development Action Plan.

Suggested Reading

Dale, Margaret, 2003. A Manager's Guide to Recruitment and Selection (MBA Masterclass Series). Kogan Page.

Payne, Tim, & Wood, Robert, 1998. Competency-Based Recruitment and Selection. John Wiley & Sons Ltd.

Cooper, D., Robertson, I., & Tinline, G., 2003. Recruitment & Selection: A Framework for Success: Psychology @ Work Series. Int. Thomson Business Press.

QUICK REFERENCE

This Quick Reference provides you with a summary of key concepts, models and reference material from Learning Short-takes®. We have also included some quotations to ponder.

Use this section as a quick reference to keep your learning active.

Quick Reference

> **Dig your well, before you're thirsty.**
>
> Harvey Mackay

The Recruitment Iceberg

Quick Reference

The Recruitment and Selection Process

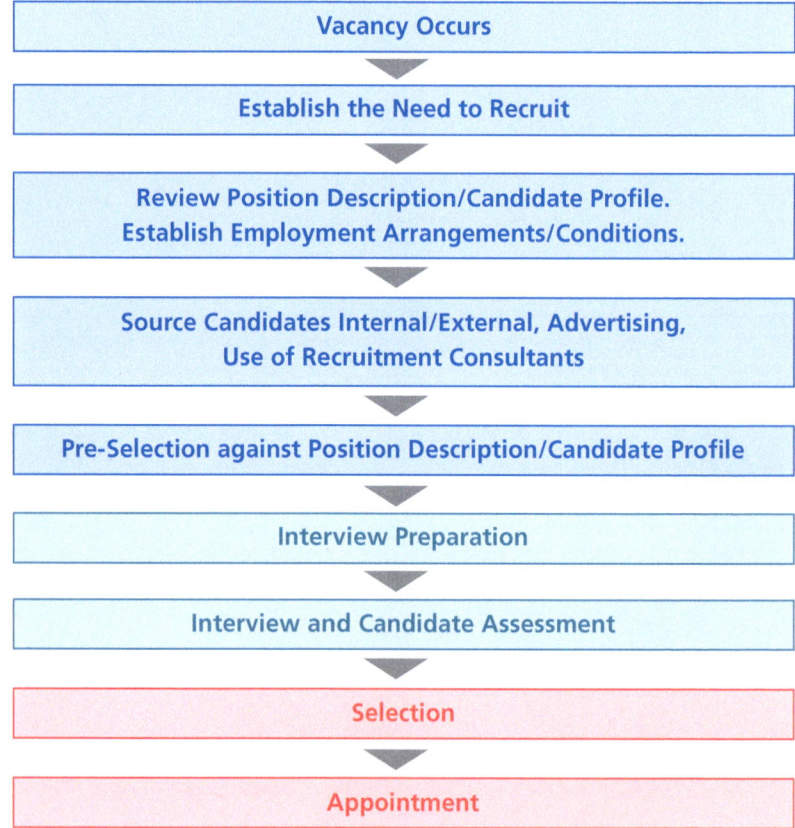

Key Considerations in Establishing a Recruitment Need

- What is the primary function of the position?
- How can the position be improved (for organisation and employee)?
- What type of person should be employed in the position?
- Can elements of the position be reallocated, modified, or eliminated entirely?
- Does the performance of the previous incumbent offer any lessons as the position's importance, effectiveness, or business impact?
- Can the position by filled internally via transfer or promotion?

Quick Reference

> **Whether you're recruiting new employees or posting jobs for internal applicants, the job description tells the candidate exactly what you want in your selected person.**
>
> Susan M. Heathfield

Determining the Requirements of the Position

Position Description

+

Candidate Profile

+

Employment Conditions

=

**Criteria for Attracting Candidates
and
Criteria for Screening Candidates**

Quick Reference

Internal Sources of Employees

- Direct appointment or promotion by management.
- Lateral transfer of an employee from one department to another.
- Internal advertising.

External Sources of Employees

- Use employee networks.
- Develop your website.
- Become an employer of choice.
- Use internet and online media.
- Utilise temporary agencies and recruitment firms.
- Capitalise on positive publicity.

Quick Reference

Critical Incident Based Interviews

> **Past performance is the best predictor of future performance.**

The STAR Model of Questioning

S / **T**	What was the **S**ituation or **T**ask?
A	What **A**ction was taken (the Behavior)?
R	What was the **R**esult (the Outcome)?

Quick Reference

Listening During the Interview

Allow the applicant to do most of the talking.
Use the 80/20 rule.

The Selection Decision

 Ensure candidates are appointed according to suitability for the position and base decisions on facts, not emotions.

Quick Reference

Top Ten Recruiting Tips

1. Improve your candidate pool.
2. Hire the 'sure thing'.
3. Look first at in-house candidates.
4. Be known as a great employer.
5. Involve your employees in the hiring process.
6. Pay better than your competition.
7. Use benefits to your advantage.
8. Hire the smartest person you can find.
9. Use your website for recruiting.
10. Check references.

NEXT STEPS

Congratulations! You have now completed this Learning Short-take® title. The entire list of Learning Short-takes® can be found on the catherinemattiske.com website.

In this section we have suggested Learning Short-take® titles for you that will build your learning. You may order these Learning Short-takes® online at https://www.catherinemattiske.com/books or from your bookstores.

Listen and Be Listened To
Transform communication in a world of distraction

Learning Short-take® Outline

combines self-study with realistic workplace activities to provide you with the key skills and techniques of effective and enhanced listening. You will learn to build more effective work relationships with your co-workers and leaders by tuning into key communication messages and responding appropriately. You will learn tips, tricks and techniques to boost active listening capability and discover that effective listening helps command respect from both the speakers and listeners point of view.

Our unique view of the world and personal style - based on our values, beliefs, attitudes and behaviors - affects how we act, perceive information, and communicate with others. It also influences the way we listen and how others listen to us. When we expect to hear certain things, we may pay attention to only what interests us. Our perception about a person, situation or subject influences our reception of information, and how much attention we choose to pay. **Listen and Be Listened To** breaks down the art and skill of active listening which is critical to building and maintaining effective working relationships.

Listen and Be Listened To includes an impactful **'Listening Tips' Wall Chart**, provided to you as a free download.

Learning Objectives

- Define listening.
- Explain why listening is important.
- Identify the barriers to effective listening.
- Identify their listening style and the listening style of others.
- Demonstrate techniques for active listening.
- Create a Skill Development Action Plan.

Course Content

- Part 1: Listening & Communication
- Part 2: Listening versus Hearing
- Part 3: Barriers to Effective Listening
- Part 4: Your Natural Listening Style
- Part 5: Passive Listening
- Part 6: Active Listening
- Part 7: Better Questions, Better Answers

Making Meetings Work
Getting the Most out of Meetings

Course Content

- Part 1: Types of Meetings
- Part 2: Why Meetings Fail
- Part 3: Solutions to Meeting Barriers
- Part 4: Planning the Meeting
- Part 5: Preparing the Agenda
- Part 6: Conducting the Meeting

Learning Short-take® Outline

Making Meetings Work combines self-study with realistic workplace activities to provide you with the key skills and techniques to make meetings work. Your meetings will become more focused, efficient, targeted and more likely to have a productive impact on the company's bottom-line. You will learn how to more effectively prepare, manage, facilitate and actively participate in meetings.

It is estimated that the average professional spends 61.5 hours per month in meetings, or two weeks every year. It is also estimated that at least 50% of this time is wasted in unproductive meeting activity. **Making Meetings Work** will provide you with the tools to help you save time and money.

Making Meetings Work includes the **Meeting Administration Checklist, Meeting Agenda** and **Meeting Minutes** provided as free downloadable tools.

Learning Objectives

- Evaluate your current level of meeting success.
- Identify the various types of meetings and explain key differences.
- Develop solutions to common meeting problems.
- Outline the steps for a successful meeting.
- Carry out meeting planning and preparation.
- Create a Skill Development Action Plan.

Influencing for Opportunity
Identify and Maximize Ways to Influence

Course Content

- Part 1: Fundamentals of Influence
- Part 2: Influence: A Choice
- Part 3: Naturally Occurring Influence Patterns
- Part 4: Methods of Persuasion
- Part 5: The Challenges of Influence
- Part 6: Building a life of Influence

Learning Short-take® Outline

Influencing for Opportunity combines self-study with realistic workplace activities to provide you with the key skills and techniques to influence those around you. You will learn the theory of influence, influence principles and strategies, as well as how to plan and prepare for important opportunities to influence. As a result, you should achieve greater results in your organization, work more productively and effectively in a team environment, and develop stronger working relationships with co-workers, suppliers and customers.

The ability to influence others is critical in today's competitive business environment. Being highly skilled in influence enables you to build the relationships you need to get results inside or outside the organization. Employees and managers alike cannot assume they have power over others - they must earn it through influence. Being an influential person is a skill that can be learned and practiced. **Influencing for Opportunity** will help you succeed in the modern corporate environment by increasing your ability to influence others.

Influencing for Opportunity includes a **toolkit of job aids and learning support tools** provided to you as free downloads.

Learning Objectives

- Identify patterns of influence.
- Evaluate how you currently use influence behaviors and identify areas for development.
- Develop influence behaviors for greater personal and business success.
- Establish clear and powerful influence goals.
- Increase influence to overcome resistance.
- Describe how to ask for and receive support.
- Design an approach for formal and informal influence situations; apply the approach to a real-life situation.
- Create a Skill Development Action Plan.

www.ingramcontent.com/pod-product-compliance
Lightning Source LLC
Chambersburg PA
CBHW042230090526
44587CB00001B/17